WHAT'S SPECIAL ABOUT SUNDAY?

Brian Edwards

Published by Day One Publications, 6 Sherman Road, Bromley, Kent BR1 3JH.

© DAY ONE PUBLICATIONS
First published 1992

ISBN 0 902548 17 4

All rights reserved. No part of this publication may be reproduced, stored in a retrieval system, or transmitted, in any form or by any means, electronic, mechanical, photo-copying, recording or otherwise, without the prior permission of Day One Publications.

WHAT'S SPECIAL ABOUT SUNDAY?

Andy. Thanks for inviting us over, Pastor. Jane and I would like your advice about something we've been discussing lately. It was triggered off by those full-page adverts in the papers a while back. I think they were put in by British Home Stores, saying they would be opening on Sundays. Isn't that against the law?

Pastor. As the law stands at present, yes it is. It is sad to see large stores advertising their intention of breaking the law. It's a bit hypocritical when they themselves put up notices in their stores that thieves will be prosecuted! As a matter of fact some B.H.S. stores have been warned in the past and, in the event, didn't open. B & Q have tried the same thing. Actually it is illegal for the newspapers to publish advertisements which encourage people to break the law!

Andy. It all seems a bit odd that in our modern society we should be arguing about what people do and don't do on Sunday. I suppose you might say: let every shop open or shut as it wants to, what does it matter?

Jane. Yes, when I've been talking about this in the office people seem to have mixed feelings. Most people I speak to are against the shops opening on Sunday, but some say to me: 'What's special about Sunday anyway?'. That's what Andy and I would like to discuss with you.

Pastor. Fine. Let's take up that question: 'What's special about Sunday?'. The best thing we can do is to go back to where it all started...

Jane. ...That must be in Exodus 20 where the fourth of the Ten Commandments says 'Remember the Sabbath day by keeping it holy'.

Andy. You're wrong there Jane. The idea of one special day in the week goes right back to the account of creation in Genesis 2. Isn't that right pastor?

Pastor. Yes, and here's a question you may never have thought of asking: Why did God take six days to create everything? After all, in the gospel stories Christ created bread, and turned water into wine instantly; he also healed limbs and cured diseases in a moment. In 1 Corinthians 15:52 Paul says that one day our bodies will be raised 'in a flash, in a twinkling of an eye'. So why didn't God create the universe in six seconds or even faster?

Andy. I must admit I've never thought of that, but since you mention it, I suppose he deliberately wanted to set us a pattern of six days work and one day rest. Let me see... yes it says here in Genesis 2:2 'By the seventh day God had finished the work he had been doing; so on the seventh day he rested from all his work.'

Jane. But surely God wasn't worn-out by the hard work of creating the whole universe?

Pastor. No, of course not. The Bible doesn't say God was tired. The word 'rested' simply means that he stopped His work of creation. Our word 'sabbath' is an English way of saying the Hebrew word for 'rested'. But God did something else, because the next verse in Genesis 2 tells us that 'God blessed the seventh day and made it holy'; which means he set this day apart as different from all the other days. So far you will notice there is no command or instruction and no reference to a special chosen people; all we have is the simple statement that this is what God did.

Andy. I wonder why God chose to set a pattern of six days work and one day rest? In other words, why did he establish a seven day week?

Pastor. That's an interesting question Andy, because this pattern of seven days doesn't fit naturally. If men had thought it up they would almost certainly have chosen a week of a different length. Notice the great creating acts recorded in Genesis 1: light, sky, dry ground, vegetation, the sun and planets, water creatures, flying creatures, animals, and finally man. That's nine divisions.

Andy. Which would give us a ten day week, or thirty-six and a half weeks in the year.

Pastor. Quick computing Andy! But a seven day week doesn't fit into the lunar year either. If you divide 365 by seven you have 52.17 weeks – that's why we have leap years every so often.

Jane. I seem to remember from my history lessons that during the French Revolution in the eighteenth century, and again during the Russian Revolution in the twentieth century, the authorities tried to change the seven day week and go metric. As you might expect it didn't work and both the French and the Russians were forced to go back to a seven day week.

Pastor. That's right Jane, and more recently it was tried in Sri Lanka, with the same result. You see, this pattern of a seven day week was part of God's creation plan. In fact, you could even say that God's last creative act was to make a seventh day and close the week.

Jane. What happened next?

Pastor. How far people followed God's pattern of six days work and one day rest we don't know, but what we do know is that by the time of the commandments you referred to earlier, God says *'Remember* the Sabbath day...'. This tells us that it was something they already knew about. In Exodus 16, when God gave the Israelites manna to eat in the desert, he told them to gather enough on the sixth day to last for the seventh day as well.

Jane. Was the keeping of the Sabbath day regarded as very important in the Old Testament?

Pastor. It certainly was. It began as a creation plan, but it became a divine commandment as well. When God built this seventh day into his creation, he didn't make it a law at first because Adam and Eve *wanted* to follow God's plans, knowing them to be the best way. But after the fall into sin men and women ignored God's plans; so God introduced Sabbath laws. This shows that the issue is very important. From then on, throughout the Old Testament, obedience to this law became a significant mark of whether or not they were trusting and following him.

Andy. But did Christ have anything to say about the Sabbath? I have heard it claimed that all the commandments are quoted by our Lord except the fourth, and so he didn't take this one too seriously.

Pastor. If anyone comes to that conclusion they could hardly get it more wrong! In fact none of the first four commandments is directly quoted by our Lord and I have not yet heard any Christian argue that we should scrap the first three! This fourth commandment is very clearly dealt with by Christ in Mark 2:27-28: 'The Sabbath was made for man, not man for the Sabbath.'

Andy. ...Ah yes, but this could mean we are free from any Sabbath regulations.

Pastor. That's a strange way to understand our Lord's words. In fact he is telling the Jews that the special seventh day had a very real value for man – it was made to help him; and the best use of it is to discover why the Lord created it in the first place. This is clear from what Christ goes on immediately to say: 'So the Son of Man is Lord even of the Sabbath'. Notice that Jesus didn't say the Sabbath was made for the Jews, or Israel or a chosen people, but for mankind generally; this means that it is for everybody's good. He was taking his hearers back, not to Exodus 20, but to Genesis 2. In fact our Lord often spoke about the Jewish Sabbath because he was sometimes accused of breaking it.

Jane. And did he?

Pastor. No, our Lord never broke even one biblical command. But the Jews added lots of their own rules to God's commandments, and it was those that Jesus often criticised. It is important to note that whenever Jesus defended his actions, he never took the opportunity to abolish the Sabbath law. In other words we can say that Jesus never cancelled the use of the Sabbath but he did correct the abuse of the Sabbath.

Andy. There are Christians who argue that since the Sabbath is part of the ceremonial law in the Old Testament, it has been fulfilled in Christ; in other words, *he* is our sabbath as we rest in the peace and reconciliation Christ gives us through his redemption. Therefore we are free from this law as we are free from all the other ceremonial laws.

Pastor. I understand the point, but Christ is not actually called our 'sabbath' in the New Testament is he? Besides, although the Sabbath day was part of the ceremonial law, it was much more than that. There were other sabbaths that God gave to his people: the Day of Atonement was one, and every seventh year was called a sabbath year; these are the sabbaths fulfilled by Christ. But the Sabbath day was part of the moral law, and, as we have seen, it was established at creation.

Andy. So we've seen that the seventh day was special because it was a plan of creation, and because it is one of the commandments, and because Christ emphasised it as well. But what is the purpose of the seventh day?

Pastor. Well, what do you think it is for?

Jane. You said earlier that the Old Testament Hebrew word for Sabbath means to rest or stop work, so I suppose that's its main purpose for us.

Pastor. That's right. The seventh day is a rest day, a day to refresh the body. God knows that we can't go on working without a break and so, just as he created the world with night following day, to give us time to rest, so he created one day in seven for a longer rest period. Professor Verna Wright, an internationally respected rheumatologist based at Leeds University, makes a strong argument that this one day rest in seven is vital for our physical well-being. This just shows how much God cares for his creation. In Exodus 23:12 where this Sabbath law is spelt out again, three different words are used. The master is told 'do not work', and that's a verb which has the same root as the word for 'Sabbath'; it means stop work. The animals are to 'rest', a word meaning to settle down and be quiet; it was a day for grazing. But the strongest word of all is reserved for the servants and visitors who are to be 'refreshed'; the word means to take a breath or be re-created or re-juvenated. So that's one purpose God has for the seventh day. Can you think of another reason?

Jane. In the list of commandments in Exodus 20 God links the seventh day with creation, so I suppose it was also a reminder that God is the creator.

Pastor. Exactly! The seventh day is not only a rest day to help the body, but a remembrance day to help the memory. In Exodus 31:17 God says the day will be a sign between himself and the Israelites because 'in six days the LORD made the heavens and the earth...'. This special day would keep reminding them of their creator. But it would remind them of something else. When the law was given a second time in Deuteronomy, God reminded the Israelites in Deuteronomy 5:15; that they had once been slaves in Egypt and he had set them free. That was intended as an incentive to care for their own servants on the seventh day, but it was also a reminder that God was their redeemer as well as their creator. So another purpose of this special day was to jog their memory. Anything else?

Jane. Not that I can think of.

Andy. I've thought of something. Didn't the Israelites double their sacrifices on the Sabbath day?

Pastor. Yes they did. In Numbers 28:9-10 the people were told to bring two lambs on the Sabbath day in *addition* to the regular burnt offering. This meant the priests had twice as much to do on this day! So the seventh day was also a worship day, to strengthen the soul. The rest was not intended to be a rest of idleness but of physical and spiritual re-creation. Probably one of the best passages in the Bible to describe the way we should or should not use this day is found in Isaiah 58:13-14, 'If you keep your feet from breaking the Sabbath and from doing as you please on my holy day, if you call the Sabbath a delight and the LORD'S holy day honourable, and if you honour it by not going your own way and not doing as you please or speaking idle words, then you will find your joy in the LORD'. Later on you may like to read together Psalm 92 which has the title: 'For the Sabbath day'. You will see there how the psalmist worships God as creator and saviour.

Andy. So these are the three reasons why God made one special day in the week, to help us to rest, remember and worship?

Pastor. There is one other reason, but it doesn't come out clearly until the New Testament. In Hebrews 4 the writer quotes from Genesis 2:2 and then from Psalm 95:11 where God warns unbelieving Jews 'They shall never enter my rest'. That is not just a reference to the Promised Land because the writer to the Hebrews goes on to say in verse 9: 'There remains, then, a Sabbath – rest for the people of God'. In other words, he uses this creation plan as a picture of the rest that believers will have in heaven. So a fourth purpose is that the special day should help believers to keep alive their hope of heaven.

Jane. Great! That gives us four good reasons to have one special day in the week: rest, remember, worship and hope. But I know some Christians who say we are not now under any Sabbath obligations because we are not under law but under grace and are free to do as we please.

Pastor. That makes the whole day sound like some terrible bondage! People who talk like that should go back to Isaiah 58:13 and see how the prophet encouraged the people to enjoy this special day, not by doing what they wanted, but by doing what God wanted. Why throw away such a wonderful gift from God? It gives us a great opportunity to rest, to remember God and worship him. Look at it this way: the law brings an obligation, but grace brings an opportunity.

Jane. But others say they don't keep Sunday special because they treat every day as a holy day.

Pastor. Yes, I've heard that pious nonsense as well Jane! Don't you think the sincere Jew in the Old Testament tried to keep all his days holy? Don't you think Isaiah himself lived a holy life all through the week? But he still had a special day. My only answer to that kind of talk is to suggest to such people that they would be wiser to keep every day like Sunday rather than treat Sunday like every other day!

Jane. But some people argue that Paul dispenses with the Sabbath day in Romans 14:5, 'One man considers one day more sacred than another; another man considers every day alike. Each one should be fully convinced in his own mind'.

Pastor. If Paul is referring to the seventh day principle, he would be overturning one of the commandments, and ignoring Genesis 2:3. But he is doing neither. Paul is referring to the holy days that men invent. He does the same in Colossians 2:16 where he warns against judging men by their observance, or non-observance, of 'a religious festival, a new moon celebration, or a sabbath day'. What Paul literally says here is 'or sabbaths'; our translations don't bring that out very well, but the apostle is thinking about special holy days, not *the* Sabbath day. In other words, if you want to celebrate Christmas Day, Good Friday, Easter Sunday, Pentecost, Harvest Thanksgiving and so on, that's alright, but don't make a law about it.

Andy. There's one subject we haven't yet mentioned. The Jews treated Saturday, the last day in the week, as the Sabbath; but we take the first day of the week, Sunday, as the special day. I have a friend at work who is a Seventh Day Adventist and he makes a lot of this. He even says you can't be a real Christian unless you follow a Saturday Sabbath rule. When and why did Christians change to Sunday as the special day?

Pastor. Apart from Paul's use of Jewish synagogue services as evangelistic opportunities, Luke 23:56 is the last reference to the followers of Christ keeping the Jewish Sabbath; here the women prepared the spices for our Lord's body but 'rested on the Sabbath in obedience to the commandment'. It is clear that those first Christians early on chose the first day of the week as their special day when they would meet to worship God. You find this, for instance, in 1 Corinthians 16:2 where Paul expected them to meet 'on the first day of every week', and from Acts 20:7 where Luke reports from Troas 'On the first day of the week we came together to break bread'. Nearly half a century later John, exiled on Patmos, referred to it as 'The Lord's Day' in a way that assumes all his readers would know what he was talking about.

Jane. But why did they change the day?

Andy. That was because the early Christians wanted to separate themselves from the Jewish way of worship. Anyway they had some great things to celebrate on the first day: it was the day on which Christ rose from the dead and the day the Holy Spirit was poured out on the church. So, every first day of the week Christians were given an opportunity to celebrate the resurrection of their Lord, without forgetting the original purpose of the Sabbath.

Jane. Yes, but can we be sure the New Testament Christians intended the first day celebrations to be a replacement for the seventh day Sabbath? I've heard it claimed that the first Sunday legislation was not brought in until the time of the Roman Emperor Constantine in the fourth century.

Pastor. That's true. In A.D. 321 Constantine, who professed to be a Christian, ordered: 'On the venerable day of the Sun, let the magistrates and people residing in the city rest, and let all workshops be closed'. But long before that, Christians had been using the first day of the week as their Sabbath day. The Christian leaders of the first few centuries were virtually unanimous in writing of the Christian use of Sunday as the special day and some even stated their disapproval of the Jewish Sabbath. An example may help you to see this. In A.D. 155 Justin Martyr described in detail a Christian Sunday service; and he also wrote a *Dialogue with Trypho*, a Jewish intellectual, in which he permitted Trypho, if he became a Christian, to go on observing the Jewish Sabbath providing he didn't expect other Christians to copy him.

Jane. So you are saying that from the Apostles onward the Christians turned the Jewish Sabbath into 'The Lord's Day' and celebrated it on the first day of the week – Sunday.

Pastor. Yes. Of course the Christians realised there were some differences between the two, just as there were differences between the Passover and the Lord's Supper, but the early church leaders only confirm what we find in Paul and John, and that is that the Christian Sunday, which they often referred to as 'the eighth day', had taken the place of the Jewish Sabbath. But in doing this they never thought of themselves as breaking the fourth commandment. Melito, the bishop of Sardis in A.D. 165, and Tertullian and Origen, Christian leaders who came later, all spoke of the 'Lord's Day' as a day of joyful celebration. In the mid third century, Eusebius, another prominent Christian leader, wrote that: 'The Word (he meant Christ) has changed and transferred the feast of the Sabbath to the rising of the light... of a true rest, the Lord's day'; and Eusebius went on to say that this is the first day of the week because on that day 'God created nothing else except the light'. As an aside, there is an interesting connection between the phrase 'The Lord's Day' in Revelation 1:20 and 'The Lord's holy day' in Isaiah 58:13. John was speaking of the Christian Sunday whilst Isaiah was speaking of the Jewish Saturday.

Jane.   Alright, I can see that we ought to keep Sunday special, and I can also see why – I can still remember those four words: rest, remember, worship and hope...

Andy.   Brilliant!

Jane.   Oh be quiet, I'm serious. What I want to know is *how* we should keep Sunday special. I've found that equally sincere Christians have different ideas about what they should or should not do on Sunday.

Pastor.   Yes they do Jane, but as usual the important thing is to get the principle right first. Some people spend so much time arguing about the practice – the how – that they lose sight of the principle – the why. The principle is that God created the seventh day and later gave commands about it. But he created and commanded for a purpose. Those four words: rest, remember, worship and hope, sum-up God's purpose. But we must always keep those words in balance. Rest doesn't mean we stay in bed all day, because then we would miss out on worship. The Christian who sleeps so late on Sunday that he can't worship with God's people or listen to the preaching, is acting contrary to God's plan just as much as the person who spends the morning digging the garden or cleaning the car.

Jane.   Can you be more specific. I understand that we must not make detailed rules about how other people should spend Sunday, but can you give some practical directions?

Pastor. Yes. First of all you ought to make sure you are properly prepared for Sunday. The Jewish Sabbath started at sunset on Friday; that meant they started to prepare for the Sabbath the evening before. I think we should do as much preparation as we can on Saturday in readiness for Sunday. You think about it Jane. There's a lot you can do. This includes getting a reasonable night's rest, and getting up in time to make sure that you arrive early and alert at church. I don't think God is pleased with the late-night party that means we grab a few hours sleep before we rush into church and settle down for a doze!

Andy. Ouch! I'm feeling a bit got at!

Pastor. Well, Andy, if the cap fits...!

Jane. Go on Pastor. Assuming we have prepared properly, how should we actually use the day?

Pastor. That's not a bad way of putting the question. The day is for our use, and the way to make the most of the day is to get into disciplined habits. A good individual and family habit is to meet regularly with God's people on the Lord's Day. This should be a habit that we never allow tiredness, holidays, relatives, examinations, or the pressure of work to interrupt. You have some good Bible support for this. Acts 2:42 shows us how eager the first century church was to worship and learn together, and Hebrews 10:25 reveals that these regular meetings were expected of the healthy Christian. It's a great day to put our study books or work reports away and clear our minds for a while of all the noise and opinions of the world. Our mind needs a rest like this, and it takes about twenty-four hours for our mental coil to unwind. Why not make it a 'no papers' and 'no telly' day? That should help to make it a delight to start with! Then, of course, as far as possible, we ought to avoid making other people work.

Jane. I suppose we could start by looking at all the jobs we don't have to do on Sunday.

Pastor. Good idea! Sunday is not a day to spend weeding the garden, cleaning the car, or improving the home, but a day to enjoy those things for the purpose they were intended. At the close of the sixth day God completed his work of creation, but he continued to enjoy what he had made. Why don't you get Sunday's milk delivered on Saturday and remember to fill up the car on Saturday night; in this way you can avoid making other people work on Sunday. Popping into the corner shop for a bag of sweets or an ice-cream is no different in principle from expecting the supermarket to be open for your weekly shop. The more different you make the day, the more enjoyable it will be, and the more benefit you will get from it. But Christians can go on discussing endlessly what they should and should not do on Sunday, whether or not they should play sport, go for a picnic, swim in the sea and so on; the best advice I can give to the Christian is that we should keep in mind those four great reasons for this special day. If we are sincerely fulfilling those then we will be keeping God's commandment. Remember, it is God we have to answer to for the way we keep his day.

Andy. I can see the value of all that for the Christian, but surely we can't expect a pagan world to follow our Christian convictions? So is it right for us to insist on laws that tell the world what it can and can't do on Sunday?

Jane. I've been thinking about that too. I believe there are a lot of odd contradictions in our present Sunday laws, for example isn't it true that the 1950 Shops Act allows you to buy a loaf of bread but not a Bible? Maybe we should scrap all the Sunday laws and let people do as they please.

Pastor. What you say about the present Sunday laws is true, Jane, but our response should not be to 'take the brakes off' but to make sure the brakes work! We need to clear up those contradictions and make sure Sunday really is a special day. You see, we are not demanding that everyone goes to church on Sunday, or even that they think about God all day, but we can insist that this one special day of rest and refreshment is good for the nation's health. There is always a penalty for those who break God's laws, and the person who tries to work seven days a week will sooner or later suffer for it. We need Sunday as a special day for the well-being of our nation, physically and socially, as well as for the important spiritual reasons.

Andy. Is that what the REST proposals are all about? Isn't REST a group who have made proposals for changing the present laws yet at the same time keeping Sunday special?

Pastor. They are not the only people trying to keep Sunday special. You may not know this, but the National Chamber of Trade, which represents one hundred and fifty thousand businesses, supports the Keep Sunday Special Campaign; so does Britain's largest retail group, the Co-operative Union. The Shopworkers' Union is also totally against Sunday trading and, according to reliable polls, nearly three-quarters of the general public are against scrapping all our Sunday laws.

Jane. So what are the REST proposals?

Pastor. Those initials stand for Recreation, Emergencies, Social gatherings and the Travelling public. The REST proposals would allow certain types of shop to open and sell all its products and others would have to stay shut and sell nothing. The 1950 Shops Act produced a list of exempt goods, that is products that could be sold on Sunday – like medicines – but it has proved almost unworkable. The REST proposals would allow categories of shops to open and sell everything they have. Those that would be allowed to open under the REST proposals include petrol stations and motor accessory shops, small general food shops, sweet shops, tobacconists and newsagents, restaurants, chemists and garden centres. The list is long, and keeps changing!

Andy. But I can see some problems in that list. These shops and centres would gain an advantage over their competitors who had to close. They could just keep extending the range of their goods; or else supermarkets would become extended garden centres! And how small is a 'small' general food shop? And if you allow motor accessories, why not bicycle shops and...

Pastor. Yes, I know, the snags are endless. To be fair though, the proposal is that a figure for square footage and the number of staff employed would dictate whether or not a shop was 'small'. Some of the REST proposals are excellent; for example they propose heavy penalties for those who advertise Sunday opening. But overall my view is that these proposals have too many loopholes that will be very quickly exploited by big business.

Andy. So, what's the answer then?

Pastor. I would suggest the best model for us to follow is Germany, where all shops are closed on Sundays; there are a few exceptions to this, like petrol stations, restaurants, cake shops, and a chemist in each area.

Incidentally shops are also closed on all but one Saturday afternoon each month. In our day of modern conveniences and fridges we really have no need for Sunday shopping and it would make Sunday really special if all shops, including garden centres, were closed. I believe that any laws trying to cobble together a compromise will soon fall into the same mess as the ones we have now. The only straightforward and effective approach is to start by ending all retail sales. It may be a bit uncomfortable at first – but we would soon get used to it.

Jane. Would you include medicines and petrol in the ban?

Pastor. No, there are some necessities and emergency services, but if the general principle is to have no trading then a few obvious exceptions are easy to control.

Jane. Is anyone putting this approach to the government?

Pastor. Very definitely. The Lord's Day Observance Society, from their offices at Bromley in Kent, have been making a strong case for a full ban on Sunday trading along the lines of the German example. My view is not that we should try to force everyone to go to church, but that everyone should be able to enjoy a national day of rest, with the exception of those involved in running essential services. That takes account of the fact that we are not a Christian nation and that people will want to enjoy the day for their own pleasure.

Andy. Couldn't it be argued that it is wrong for the government to legislate on what people should and should not do on a Sunday? This is supposed to be a free country isn't it?

Pastor. I'm sure some people would argue like that. But remember, governments already force us to do a lot of things that they consider will be for our good: like wearing seat belts and crash helmets, and not smoking marijuana or taking hard drugs, and closing pubs at a reasonable hour of the night and so on. Sometimes there has to be legislation to keep people free. Our government has a duty to ensure that the nation is protected from its own folly, and a seven-day working week is both sinful, because it is against God's command, and foolish, because it is against the nations' own best interests.

Jane. I see. You draw a distinction between legislation that allows people the freedom not to work and legislation that tells people what they must do with their freedom.

Pastor. Yes, that's right. I support the first but not the second. If a man spends the whole day occupied with his hobby or sport rather than worshipping God then he is answerable to God, not to me or anyone else, but at least we must ensure he has the opportunity both to rest and worship.

Jane. On the other hand people should not be allowed to spend the day with their hobby or sport in such a way that others lose their right to keep Sunday special.

Pastor. Remember, and this is important, it is not the shoppers nor the shopworkers who want the stores to be open on Sunday. That's a fact. The pressure comes from the Shopping Hours Reform Council which is a lobby made up of the really big retail boys like the Kingfisher Group, B & Q, Texas, W.H. Smith and Payless. Since 1986 the Shopping Hours Reform Council has been after total deregulation – which means anybody can open and sell anything.

Jane. But if that happens it means every day of the week would be the same constant routine. Family and social activities would be almost impossible to arrange and hundreds of thousands of people would not be free to rest or gather together for worship or friendship. That must be bad for us as a nation!

Pastor. That's right Jane. But don't forget that this is not just about shops and stores opening on Sunday. More and more businesses are trying to make employees work on Sunday, and we must strongly oppose this as well – in all but essential cases. Remember, Andy and Jane, that this one day of rest each week is God's best plan for us all – whether we are Christians or not – so we must show people, positively, what a delight this special day can be.